Oh say can you Seed?

I'm the Cat in the Hat,
and I think that you need
to come take a look at
this thing called a seed.

The Cat in the Hat's Learning Library™
introduces beginning readers to basic non-fiction. If your child can read these lines, then he or she can begin to understand the fascinating world in which we live.

Learn to read. Read to learn.

This book comes from the home of

THE CAT IN THE HAT
RANDOM HOUSE, INC.

*For a list of books in **The Cat in the Hat's Learning Library**, see the back endpaper.*

The editors would like to thank
BARBARA KIEFER, Ph.D.,
Charlotte S. Huck Professor of Children's Literature,
The Ohio State University, and
PATRICIA JONAS, Director of Library Services,
Brooklyn Botanic Garden,
for their assistance in the preparation of this book.

Visit us on the Web!
www.randomhouse.com/kids
www.seussville.com

Educators and librarians, for a variety of teaching tools, visit us at
www.randomhouse.com/teachers

Library of Congress Cataloging-in-Publication Data
Worth, Bonnie.
Oh say can you seed? : all about flowering plants / by Bonnie Worth ;
illustrated by Aristides Ruiz.
   p. cm. — (The Cat in the Hat's learning library) Includes index.
ISBN 978-0-375-81095-4 (trade) — ISBN 978-0-375-91095-1 (lib. bdg.)
1. Plants—Juvenile literature. 2. Seeds—Juvenile literature. [1. Flowers. 2. Seeds.]
I. Ruiz, Aristides, ill. II. Title. III. Series.
QK49 .W73 2001 580—dc21 00-059108

Printed in the United States of America
25 24 23 22 21 20 19 18

Oh say can you Seed?

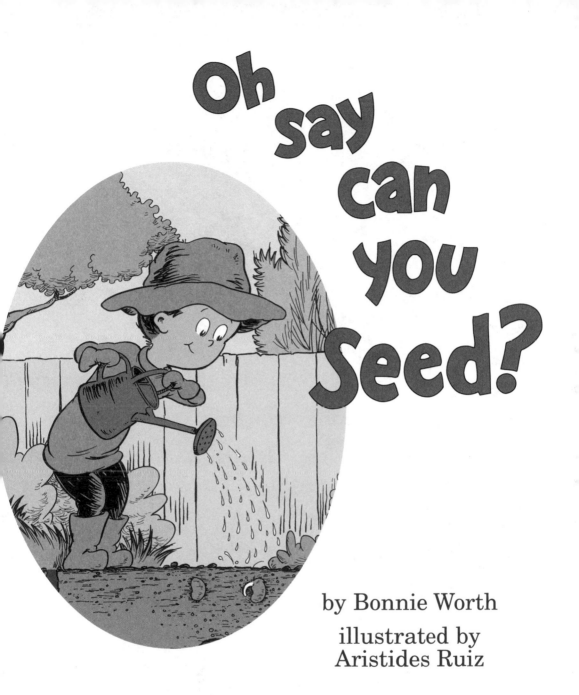

by Bonnie Worth

illustrated by
Aristides Ruiz

The Cat in the Hat's Learning Library™

Random House 🏠 New York

I'm the Cat in the Hat,
and I think that you need
to come take a look at
this thing called a seed.

From the giant gum tree
to this very small weed,
every flowering plant
started out as a seed.

Plants are so useful
to me and to you.
Can you think of the ways?
I will name you a few.

The paper for books and
the cloth for your pants
came from trees and from cotton—
that's two kinds of plants.

The grains and the fruits
and the veggies you eat—
why, they come from plants, too.
And here's something neat . . .

In deserts and woods
and rain forests thick
grow plants that can make
you feel well when you're sick!

Yes, plants serve us well
and fill so many needs,
and flowering plants
all started as seeds.

Just what is a seed,
you are wondering, maybe
Well, you might say a seed
is a tiny plant baby!

The best way for you
to see just what I mean
is to take a close look
at a seed called a bean.

Like all seeds, a bean
comes in three basic parts.
Thing One and Thing Two,
please bring on the charts!

Part one is the first that
I think you should know:
it's the part that's the baby.
It's called em-bry-o!

EMBRYO

BEAN SEED

To sprout, it needs food,
like you and I do,
which brings us to
seed part numero two.

14

It's called cot-y-le-don.
Say, isn't that fun?
This bean seed has two,
but some others have one.

cotyledon

BEAN SEED

COAT

BEAN SEED

THIN 1 G

Last comes the third part
that you need to know.
It's the coat, which protects
our cute bean embryo.

To sprout a bean seed,
keep it moist, but not wet.

Keep it covered with dirt
and then see what you get.

n seven or so days
omes the part that I love:

STEM

ROOT

a root spreads below
and a stem shoots above.

17

Now, in order to show a
grown bean plant to you,
we've traveled in time
for some months. Maybe two.

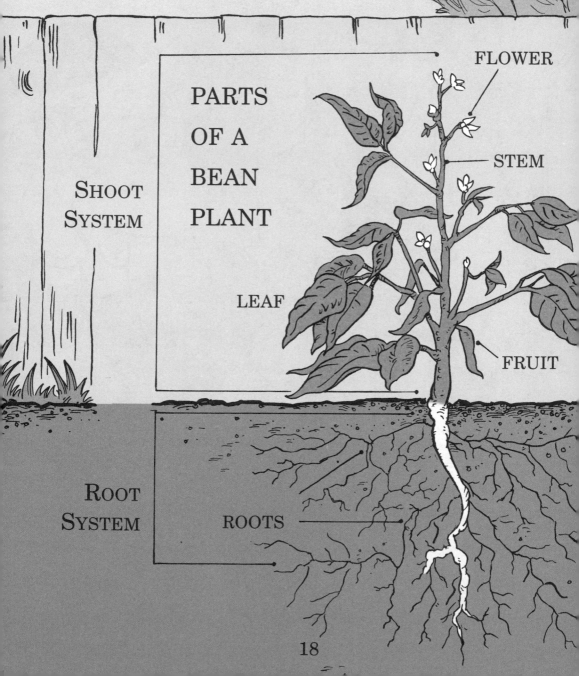

PARTS
OF A
BEAN
PLANT

SHOOT
SYSTEM

ROOT
SYSTEM

FLOWER

STEM

LEAF

FRUIT

ROOTS

Thing Two calls the part
aboveground the shoot system.

Thing One calls the part
underground the root system.

To get a good look at the
roots underground,
it is better to make like
a mole, I have found.

Roots are not pretty.
They're twisty and hairy.
And some roots look even
a little bit scary!

Roots anchor a plant
and help it stand true.
Roots suck up the water
and minerals, too.

20

And roots keep the soil
from just washing away.
That's pretty important,
now, wouldn't you say?

We've talked about roots.
We have learned about them.
Now it is time we
moved on to the stem.

The stem is a pipe
through which water shoots.
It's absorbed from the soil
and passed up through the root

It shoots through the plant,
and next (as you'll see)
the leaves each turn into
a food factory!

Just like the rhino's
protected with horns,
the stem of a rose
is protected with thorns.

23

Leaves come in all shapes
and all sizes, I've found—
some small and some spiky,
some big and some round.

SMOOTH
EDGES

NARROW
LEAVES

TOOTHED
EDGES

WAVY
EDGES

But the thing that all leaves
have in common is this:
they make their own food
by pho-to-syn-the-sis.

LOBED
EDGES

I'll say this quite loudly—
I don't mean to be rude—but . . .

BROAD,
FLAT LEAVES

PLANTS ARE THE ONLY
LIVING THINGS ON EARTH
THAT MAKE THEIR OWN FOOD!

To do this, plants need
water, minerals—and sun.
And that's why the daytime's
when food-making's done.

SHRINK - UPPER

For your information—
and also for fun—
hop in my Shrink-Upper
and let's see how it's done.

The leaf takes in CO_2*
through a stoma, or pore.
It works like a mouth,
and that's what it's for.

Then the air gets mixed in
with the water and sun.
And that's how the
food-making factory is run!

(*Carbon dioxide.)

SUNLIGHT

= FOOD

STOMA

CO_2 ENTERS
THROUGH STOMA
ON UNDERSIDE
OF LEAF.

WATER

I see by my clock
that now is the hour
to drop in and say a
hello to the flower!

OXYGEN

Plants breathe out a gas
that we breathe in.
The name of that gas
is OX-Y-GEN!

INSIDE

FOOD

29

Thing Two has a chart—
he will share it with you—
that shows what the parts
of a flower all do.

PARTS OF A FLOWER

POLLEN GRAIN

STAMEN
└ ┌ ANTHER
  └ FILAMENT

PETAL

STIGMA
STYLE
OVARY

PISTIL

POLLEN
TUBE

OVULE

In the pistil are ovules—
they're unfertilized seeds.
The stamen holds pollen,
which an ovule needs.

30

An unfertilized ovule
will not ever grow,
and pollen's the stuff
that will fix that, you know.

(A flower's own pollen
or another's okay.)
That's where the bees
play a role, by the way.

To make honey, bees need
to get nectar from flowers.
They fly and they gather
this sweet stuff for hours.

The pollen sticks onto
their bodies and legs.
It falls off and, sometimes
it reaches the eggs!

An ovule that's fertilized
becomes a seed.
Around it grows fruit,
upon which we feed.

When we say the word "fruit,"
do you know what that means?
It means olives, nuts, grains,
plantains, tangerines!

And apples and oranges
and pineapples, too—
all kinds of plant foods
that are healthy for you.

Some fruits are juicy
and messy to munch on.
Dry ones, like nuts,
are nice just to crunch on.

Not all plants with seeds
give us edible fruit.
Some plants have seeds
that look weird or look cute.

Bur seeds are hitchhikers
that ride on your clothes.
And dandelion seeds
sometimes fly up your nose.

Some seeds come in pods
that explode like a sneeze.
Other seeds may have wings
and can fly on a breeze.

But whether they stick
or they blow or they fly,
seeds bring us life,
and now you know why.

I see the sun setting and
here comes the moon.
Your mother is calling.
Your dinner is soon.

hope you have learned
from my little seed talk.
And now I will climb up . . .

. . . this giant beanstalk!

GLOSSARY

Carbon dioxide: The gas humans and animals breathe out, and which green plants use to make food.

Cotyledon: The first leaf or pair of leaves within the embryo. A part of the seed that stores food.

Edible: Fit to eat.

Embryo: The part of a seed that develops into a new plant, including the stem, leaves, and roots.

Fertilization: When the male (or sperm) cells contained in pollen reach the female (or egg) cells in the ovules and cause them to grow into seeds.

Minerals: Materials that are neither animal nor vegetable. Found in rocks and soil, they can help animals or plants to grow.

Nectar: The sweet liquid secreted by a flower to attract pollinators like bees, butterflies, and hummingbirds.

Numero: The Spanish word for "number."

Ovule: The part of the plant in the ovary that contains egg cells and becomes a seed after fertilization.

Oxygen: The gas humans and animals must breathe in order to stay alive, and which green plants produce when making food.

Photosynthesis: The process by which green plants, powered by the energy of sunlight, combine carbon dioxide and water to produce sugar inside their leaves and release oxygen into the air.

Pistil: The ovule-bearing, female reproductive part of a flowering plant that includes the stigma, style, and ovary.

Plantain: A kind of banana that is best eaten when cooked.

Pollen: The minute grains that are produced in the anthers of a flower and contain male sex cells.

Stamen: The male reproductive part of a flowering plant that includes the anthers and the filaments that support the anthers.

FOR FURTHER READING

A Weed Is a Flower by Aliki (Simon & Schuster, *Aladdin Paperbacks*). Tells the fascinating true story of Dr. George Washington Carver, a son of slaves who became internationally famous for his work with plants. For grades 1 and up.

How Do Apples Grow? by Betsy Maestro, illustrated by Giulio Maestro (HarperTrophy, *Let's-Read-and-Find-Out Science*®, Stage 2). All about apples—from flowers to fruit! For grades 1 and up.

I Am a Leaf by Jean Marzollo, illustrated by Judith Moffatt (Scholastic, *Hello Reader! Science*™—Level 1). A leaf on a maple tree explains photosynthesis. For preschool through grade 1.

One Bean by Anne Rockwell, illustrated by Megan Halsey (Walker and Company). Step-by-step instructions on how to grow a bean plant. For preschoolers and up.

INDEX

The Cat in the Hat's Learning Library™